PHRASES OF LONESOME DAYS

SILENT DREAMS

HANLOLA Y ESTHER

Made with ♥ on the Notion Press Platform
www.notionpress.com

For my Parents,

and for all the people who believed in me.

Contents

Contents

Contents

Acknowledgements

I thank Heavens for guiding me till this day
and Earth for bearing its beauitiful Earthlings.

Phrases of Lonesome Days

silent Dreams

Hanlola Y Esther

1. Chapter-1

There'll be a spring
where our dreams will bloom
its you, how you wish to plant
and enjoy the blossom.

2. Dreams of Blooms

I'm longing for spring,
got dreams of blooms.
Death roses..?,
no, tears of rain had em' bath.
Blooms of roses..?,
yes thats what i yearn.
You se, as i clasp tighter,
thorns on it hurts heart.
Blood and tears drops deeper,
but i got em'to strengthen,
my roots of dying roses.
Making deeper deep roots.
Patience for passionate bloom.
Less care about the colours.

3. Perseverance

Then i was eleven,
get a whiff of printed pages.
Filling every empty pages,
with phrases and rhymes.
Ink on all my tiny fingers,
striving to create fancies on blank pages.
No man to address to set my fascination.
Lost all alone,
to see my imaginations on screen,
to see my thoughts on printed pages.
Years overpass without a single triumph.
Yet the perseverance i had didn't die,
creating in my mind more than ever.
Trusting my inner will, to make it
one day.

4. Dazzling star Damozel

To the dazzling star damozel,
endowed with crown of love.
Gracious lilies of star,
empress of patience and kindness.
Let thy heart allay with tears,
the broken pieces of your heart.
Let the aura of your tears,
aromatized thy broken heart.
Oh beautiful damozel dear,
spruce up thy blessed armour mildly.
Thrive out as sunshine brights up,
you don't waste to stay weak.
Love of heavens and Earth damozel,
ascend oh dear beautiful damozel.

5. Rise up Girl

Rise up, held your head high.
Race up, keep your head awake.
Be the one to fly high.
Let your mind race as time ticks.
Rise in colours of rainbow,
build thy empire alone.
Paint your paints in colours.
Keep racing and shine above all.
Make thy dream worth dreaming,
save no ears for naysayers.
Keep a space for thyself worth,
let your imaginations be seen.

6. Chapter-2

I thought
why long for heaven when love is next to me
but alone.. i go through hell,
to be with you.

7. Dear Honey

Dear honey,
A letter from your by-and-by wife,
that my dearest. I can no longer dream
to be your bride in veil.
All i want is nothing then to let you go,
Be yourself and live in ecstasy,
smile whenever
send empty mails.
Dear you aren't a bird in an aviary
that i drive you to sleep,
cook together dine together
i can't tussel everytime to make you
as a man i want.
be youself for i'm not the one all along.

8. Letter to In-Laws

Before our acquaintances,
let me speak of me.
My name as you know,
my persona you would learn.
To be a radio,
coversations i lack.
My honour and love would be showed as you deserve.
In days to come and years together.
When i fail a work,
i forbid not point my parents,
they nurtured me well.
It is i who would play my role.
Let me do what i can.
When i fail, let me learn.
when i wrong, correct my path.
And i would be a lady thou all
dream an In-Law to be.

9. The Incense

'Do you still have the incense,
my mothers choice i packed.
Could you burn it, the incense,
and let the ardour spell
and wake our innocent hearts.
When i handed it to you
it meant alot more.
I'm lying cold alone,
deep down your ground.
Wake me up whisper my name.
Call my name, burn the incense.
Your warm arms are afar.
Everythings fading from my sight,
i'm waiting your call,
as i'm not ready to leave alone.
Wake me up whishper my name.
Call my name, burn the incense.

10. December Ride

Do you remember Honey,
that cold december ride,
how i felt so alive,
rhyming along your heartbeat.
Our hearts attached from that moment.
In the mid-night of our ride,
when the moon beams in,
you brush my brown shinny hair gently,
then kiss on my forehead.
That mark the sign of our union in love.
Now golden years had passed,
and my brown hair to grey,
on my last brethe i wish to you,
to kiss me at the stroke of mid-night,
a sign of our everlasting love.
To mark our golden years together.
To rewind our first ride together.

11. Four Summers and Winter

In love we pass four summers,
then celebrated four winters,
and on fourth spring we ended,
almost close to matrimony.
It was only a trial,
Never put to test,
if we could endure the separation.
A sudden end to our four lovely years.
Tried a little hard, but failed.
My heart couldn't hold on.
Almost your lady, showed all my heart.
Yet you couldn't afford it,
to give your affections to me.
In love we pass four summers and winters,
and on fourth spring we ended.

12. This Feelings

Oh this feeling.,!
Even when you sit next to me,
i can't help thinking of you.
Even when you are mine,
i wish you to be mine for forever.
I did't know when,
how i fall into,
yet pretty sure, i have fallen so far.
Maybe you'll never see it.
Maybe you'll never acknowledge it.
But someday i might settle in your mind and never leave.

13. Deep Inside

Deep inside.,
I wish somebody to look at me,
the way i do.
Pat my hair,
brush my hair,
hold my hand.
smile at me.
Yet i want that somebody to be only you.
Simple wishes,
yet like a rare gem,
i never get it,
and you never do it,
And so i do it to you,
and my heart still melts.

14. The Groom

Twas a fall of merry bells bash.
A newly wedded pair,
the Bride awaiting for her Groom's homecoming.
Her love in suit went to earn a bread for em'.
The Bride awaits in sunshine,
untill gloomy sky poured rain.
As women panics in terror,
she hears the mourns of dead.
Her groom faced a massacre,
a newly bond destroyed by fate.
As Bride mourns in rain,
the Grooms soul fades in fog,
promising to wait in another land,
where noone would harm their fate.

15. Chapter-3

I hope our Guardian Angels knows,
our helplessness to sin,
that makes someone else happy.

16. The Contrition

Never by my sins,
should my parents mourn.
Never by my sins,
should they endure heartpains.
For my sins,
pour all curse on me.
In darkness i dwell.
I delayed to turn back in light.
Yet even when i'm late,
i would still wish my parents happinesse.
Would pray for e'm even,
when i'm blind by darkness.

17. Forbidden Sin

Lord again and again i sin,
the forbidden sin,
that i forbid never to sin again.
The forgiven sins.
The sin so beautiful,
that i fail to escape from it.
Something so lovely,
that lures everyone.
Now i owe my soul for your mercies,
and i want your light,
to close my eyes from the beautiful sin.

18. Love and Sins

Love, the sweetness in her flower.
Sin, the burden to his soul.
Love, that appreciates her flaws.
Sin he hates, but the deed he does.
All for love, sin for love.
Hard to please love and deject sin.
She cries for her soul.
He cries for his love.
Twas, love that made her joy,
and twas sin that made her cry.
The purity in his soul,
was the love she felt for.

19. Chapter-4

We converse all night in my head,
and you stares at me like i'm the brightest star,
and that's why,
i never wana come back from my thoughts.

20. Lets Runaway

Is it her fault,
to fall in love with you,
when she knows, she's betrothed.
Should i blame the universe,
or fate,
or destiny.
She knows you'll never be hers,
and she'll never be yours.
But a fake hope will do.
Lets Runaway, faraway,
an unnamed cafe,
across the sea,
watching the seagulls.
smiling like forever,
holding hand in hand,
that's her daydream.

21. The Red Handkerchief

There's a little man,
wiping all of the sweat.
His hands running up and down,
dress like a Grim reaper,
with a red handkerchief,
he wipes the sins for souls.
When my fate met him,
he hypnotized me in madness of happiness,
singing i'm a murderer, a sinner.
Yet he wipes away with smile.
My fair soul is locked and my dark soul rules.
Yet when he appeared he set my fair soul free.
A knock on my heart and a kiss on a cheek,
crack the dark door and my fair soul's free.

22. The World and the Dream

The world, a place i live.
The Dream, a place he live.
A leading character in my dream.
We drift apart when daylight shines.
Between our world, there's a wall,
when night comes he takes me to his world,
call 'Dream' thats behind the wall.
We dance under the moon,
ride over the galaxies,
shooting stars like jets,
play all over the clouds.
But when i wake up,
everything disappears and i'm beneath the wall.
The world i live has nothing like in the land of 'Dream'.

23. Chapter-5

Unrequited
And all of the love we love,
the love you find so pure is always an unreqited love.

24. Unrequited Love

How to i describe
this theory of attraction.
I don't intend to look.
I don't intend to hit.
But you crosses my mind,
everytime i think of my day.
I hate it for i'm carrying it alone,
this unrequited feelings.
A false alarm rings my instinct,
an invisible magnetism pulls me,
atracting your every moment.
How to i find this equation,
when i donot know,
this theory of unrequited attractions.

25. Another Day Again

Its another day again,
watching you stand there,
mesmerized by your look,
trying not to freak
when your eye meets mine.
The cold breeze blowing my hair,
a drizzle and a soft wind,
then i imagine my favourite song with you.
From rushy cloud, i can see you standing.
From the noisy crowd, i hear my heart thumbs, as i see you.

26. Love in vain

All my efforts all my time in vain.
Wrote lines in your name, seek your turn.
The way you sweetly care' melt me.
Bought music strings,
gave you melodies,
composed love songs.
But you weren't ready.
all you want, was my time and attentions,
but you never reciprocate it.

27. There you go

There you go.
I watched you glow day by day.
Waited for a moment to tell you.
I watched you smile graciously.
pretty days passed and passed by.
Keep silent,celebrate your glow.
When my heart gets heavier i wanted to spell out.
But then,
there you go, gaily and jolly,
walking with your love.
Now i watched you smile graciously,
walking hand in hand with her,
I watched you long ago,
but now that you look happy i'll stay silent.
I'll watched you from behind,
untill you keep that smile,
i'll cheerish you,
from the soft corner of my heart.

28. Stars to Butterflies

Aren't you fatique of perampulating
in my head.
Each night you keep me awake.
Lost from my state.
I see night stars all butterflies.
A flying kiss from firelies.
Blush in my sleep,
smiles on my face,
thanks to my dreams,
for its always in my dream i feel that dazzles.

29. Heaven's curse

An atheist i was, stark.
Dead, yet alive in dark.
Never knew heavens heard me.
Never knew pains taught me.
I condemned heaven's for distress and pains,
yet heaven's curse me with love.
Unwitting about the curse,
heedlessly detached heart falls in,
twas an unseen and unnamed person.
He appeared without a warning,
showed how living in light feels.
Yet disappeared without a word.
And i'm lost in between light and dark.

30. Winter Night

Flashback to cold december night,
an outlander gazing in my eyes.
I attend heed to his conscious,
enchanted by the look he gave,
i stand still, bewitch by his charm.
After a glance he vanish in crowd.
Never knew if i was hallucinating,
or the real figure.
and now every winter,
i wish to see him again.

31. Chapter-6

You offered me a rose,
you never mentioned about those thorns that hurts.

32. Roller Coaster

My love on roller coaster,
you swing me high and low,
you appear and disappear
whenever you wish.
Take me in or
push me out.
I'm tired of standing at your door,
you kept your door ajar and
never once open widely for me.

33. Before I'm Yours

Before I'm yours,
and before we wed.
May i do what i do,
may i sleep when I'm tired.
Before our hearts are bind as one,
let me brethe,
let me live,
let me sing, my own melody.
Before I'm yours I'm mine.
And even when I'm yours,
I'll be my ownself
and not loose myself pleasing you.

34. Tyrant lover

A weary young man passed the path,
with a heart pierced,
walking with a lifeless soul.
He forbears from the path,
walked downd my passage.
Seeing my freedom he called.
Take me to your world,
i long for purity,
a soul tied by a tyrant lover.
I tarried seeing his avid serene,
I say,
'spread your wings and hover up,
i'll clasp and profer my warm hands,
when you dive down.'

35. Like 'Spring

Like spring you changed,
like the season changed.
You were in me for time,
i was in you for long.
You gave me flowers in my heart,
your fragnance in my soul,
the smell that stuck in me.
You made my heart warm,
held my hand close,
now feelings fade cold as season changed.
Like spring your feelings changed.
In spring ,you gave me flowers,
and in autumn your feelings fades.

36. Freedom over chain

A life of freedow i prefer,

but you chain me with your smiles.

I long to disappear,

but waits for your search.

I keep trying to flee afar,

yet my heart reluctant.

I have seen the fallouts,

i donot intend to fall the same.

I owe you for every happiness you gave,

i would repay in flowers of regrets.

I want freedom over a golden chain.

i'm chain in a golden cage,

but no matter how much happiness it gives,

i'm still in a cage,

and so i choose freedow over chain.

37. 'She's not scared

She's not scared of letting you go,
she's scared of loosing the part of her that grew in you.
She's scared,
memories will hunt.
Scared of loving someone new,
scared to give her heart again,
to rebond with someone not from her dreams.
Everytime she closes her eyes,
and accept your imperfections.
All she want is your affections,
and she'll make it right the rest.

38. 'I died'long Ago

I died long ago,
but it still hurts,
i'm out of tears,
my emotions all numb.
Like a parent who abandons a child,
so you,
a lover who suck my soul empty
and abandoned.
My soul is drain,
like a drought in my soul,
i died long ago in many ways,
you suck all the sweetness in me,
and now not even tears would fall.

39. The Blame

Broken heart she lay,
every night on wet pillows.
cotton soaked in tears,
insecurities all over her mind,
wishing for amnesia.
Devastating, breathing hard, sobbing.
When love fails all blames on her.
Now too scared of attachments,
waving off every perfect man,
cause men are all men.
Scared to loose, the little part of her that remain,
for she loose the part of her in you.
With teary eye she lay,
watching the moon go blur,
as she looses her breathe slowly.

40. Chapter-7

Soulmates aren't always lovers,
it can be your bestfriends,
your family,
and people you adore.

41. A Brave blood

I write the lines and poems all for my king,

for the worthy and loyalty, for his bravery.

He pour his blood and tears to build his kingdom.

He works tiredlessly, from dusk till dawn.

He is our king , we call him 'Father.

Our family is the kingdow he cares for.

His bravery belives in his daughters.

He values all his childrens, taught his daughters that,

a wise woman can led the whole folk, better than man.

He knows one day, his daughters,

would prove his blood bravely,

and create a home a better one,

42. Dear 'Beloved

All the seasons,
spring and fall pass by.
Summers and winters ,
every season pass by.
Its quite long,
you never ever return,
not even in my dreams.
Your sweet footprints cheerish and praise.
Your deeds remains.
Memories still linger,
windy and cold nights feels nothing,
when i miss you in silent tears.
You left without a word,
still miss, still love, still hope
to meet you in another life,
to fulfill our promises.
We still feel your prsence in our midst,
i hope you're hovering up there,
as the brightest sky.

43. My Father's love

Not a word i find to describe my father's love.
Tender and compassionate,
humple and loving,
caring and passionate.
Not a word i find to describe his love.
I belive there's Man who is simple and humble,
kind and tender,
and that's what i know from my Father,
that Good Man does exist,
and not every Man is cruel.

44. Dearest Father

My dearest Father,

Thy darling daughter here,

i botched to be thy child of innocence.

I'm cloaked with dirt in fear.

Thy darling daughter isn't virtous,

i long how affectionate thou call my name.

The love you accord was all enough, but remain vicious.

My rigid heart, wreck phantasm, i shame.

You nurtured me sweetness and love.

Yet the love of other man bestowed bitterness and shame.

He lured me with heart of sweetness,

and destroyed my happiness with his sweetness.

Breathing my last moments, while i write,

as i failed to bear the heartpains of betrayals.

How preciuos your tears to weep for me.

When ye wake up, i'll be asleep,

as i drift off to peaceful sleep,

i wish you be my father again in another life.

45. Back Home

Back Home,
i can imagine the scenes,
mom's there dad's there,
growing grey,
laughing at silly jokes of my siblings.
Oh i love them,
so dearly, hold on my home,
i'm battling, i'm working
to get to there,
to be with ya'll.
I miss the smell of tress and hills,
smoke from our chimmney,
and warm meals together.

46. Apa' An Angel

Apa' here's your unfaithful child,
shamelessly kneel, to beg your forgiveness.
I was an evil who tore your hopes,
made you cry, made you lost your nights.
I turn your love to despair,
you fed me love yet i gave you hard days.
You wipe your tears aside,
and show your smile.
But now i see the sadness in your eye behind your smile.
Little did i know, you were an Angel on earth.
You guided me, loved me, and forgave me.
You're my Angel.

47. A magic portrait

Your captured smile in a portrait
takes me back to gaily days.
Across bloom rhododentrons, we run,
plucked and squeezed to pink and purple,
whistling, ringing alone the birds.
Your captured smile in a portrait, looks so alive,
takes me back to days we walk holding our hands.
You were my soul twin,
i lost you and my soul's weak.
How i wish time machines, magic compass,
magic clock take me into magic portrait,
that'll all take me to you.

48. Chapter-8

And what if you never wake up tommorow,
who would do the things you dream about,
do it now or nevermore.

49. Anymore or Nevermore

A sudden thought woke my dreaming sense,
i laid my pen down to jot every wish.
Pour every emotions with ink.
I lay on my sick bed.
Between death and life,
the thought in me woke me,
to do things i dream,
now or nevermore.
I donot know when my breathe would stop,
and so i'll do now the things to do now,
or would never get to do nevermore.

50. Do not call me 'Dead

Do not call me death,
when i breathe nomore.
Do not call me late,
when i stand no more.
For i'll live in words.
When i breathe nevermore,
my name shall breathe e'ermore.
Ink of silver, on marbles,
with ardour of craft,
the words i write on marbles.
Draw a castle of witch craft,
then rhyme along the spells.
Run with rhymes from misery.
Into another dimension i dwell.
Reach me, keep me in your shelf.
I shall live,
in words, in books,
and my name shall rhyme e'ermore.

51. Still '18

The face of adulthood hit the year of '18,
calmness in isolation i find peace.
Patience i lack to stay in crowd of folk.
The rise and failure, experiences and pains
stroke me and i failed to wake up.
It paused the time of my growth,
and now years passed yet i still feel '18.
Like years never changed after i last stand in crowd.
Somethings never change,
and i'm afraid to face the same,
like im stroke with year of '18 experiences.
As i feel im still '18.

52. Traumatic childhood

My childhood was traumatic,
by my own creation of thoughts,
the fear to face the world,
lingered between reality and dreams.
Never been myself,
numerous characters i create live in me.
Every character showed ways,
to deal with the people.
My childhood was a mess,
a traumatic childhood,
seen things never to be seen.
Not sure which character defines the real me.

53. Noises in me

The noises in me,
fails me to talk.
The words in my mind,
yet fails to speak out.
I wish you jolly in my head,
i greet you well in my head,
but it never work out in actions,
only if you could read my mind, i do wish i'm cheerful.
It's too noisy in my head,
and my mind up on minding
the noises in silent.
But i can't bring out in actions.

54. Chapter-9

Life is like colours of roses, lily and peony,
depends on how you grow
and which suits you.

55. My Life before

I think i lived a life before,
even before this life.
May this life never had love,
yet i had trauma's of heartbreaks.
I had a life before,
had a love before,
and i know how it ends,
and this life knows nothing.
Everything i do feels 'dejavu',
this life knows nothing but my soul does.
I lived a life before
yet i donot know who i was.
I know how things look without stepping out,
not me my soul does,
nothing feels like a first time,
but like living in someone else identiy.

56. Politics and i don't go along

Politics and i don't go along.
But may i note what i see,
How people assure to serve you,
and you trust them, give the will,
and when they sit on a throne,
they stand on your head.
And your turn to criticize,
you choose for greed they spread,
and you blame them,
aren't you the one who choose them
to stand on your head,
and obey their will.
Don't you think you would do same,
when you are in their shoe with power to corrupt.

57. The Best page

My journey and journal in one book,

of different chapters and pages,

above all the best page i adore,

is a late childhood and early youth.

Free from responsibilities,

fly around all edges.

Their names in 'K',

a key to my happiness.

Noone knows untill when,

we'll fly crazy and free.

Sing together, stay up late,

close our eyes,and walk the road.

Everything was a mess of joy,

plans made like we'll be together forever.

Walk together in every rainstorm,

do crazy little funs.

But life isn't same now,

we grew up,

responsibilities of our own life on our shoulders.

Scattered, dispersed old days never come back,

yet we have piles of memories to look at and smile.

58. Youth and Spring

Life's a season,
youth's a spring.
The beauty of youth is a beauty of spring.
No alarm of autumn falls,
no dread of end.
The blooming age captivated by every passer ring.
Mesmerized by beauty of blossom,
yet the youth in life for once,
though spring come and go,
Youth never comes back,
for life's like a single year,
And so enjoy every season of life.

59. Money and fame

Person of money and fame,
got friends of all kind.
Money give riches,
And riches build fame.
But would a hardwork beats off,
they say money means nothing,
but creativity means everything,
but don't you know money buys eveything.
But ironically
A person full of talent lacks money, that builds fame.
And person of wealth lacks creativity.
And in between hardwork beats off.

60. Little Foundlings

Five little foundlings singing their own ditty,
one little toddler as hard as his tongue could ditty.
They call themselves full-blown.
Gathered from diverese broken hearths.
Cheer thier songs in one hearth.
The melancholic tone covers the scenario,
singing along the eldest, O Henrio'.,
Their parents gave em' life,
yet care no more their existence.
For all five foundlings,
only a Granny to look after em'
She watch em' grown in symphony'
run after their mischieves.
Singing when their hearts sink,
seeing other boys with their mama's,
All they do is hold their hands and sing,
Lulling the little toddler not to weep,
for they are together.

www.ingramcontent.com/pod-product-compliance
Lightning Source LLC
Chambersburg PA
CBHW050806160726
48004CB00002B/727